MW00834779

BÔ YIN RÂ

THE BOOK
ON
HAPPINESS

BÔ YIN RÂ
(J. A. SCHNEIDERFRANKEN)

THE BOOK
ON
HAPPINESS

TRANSLATED BY
B.A. REICHENBACH

THE KOBER PRESS
SAN FRANCISCO, CALIFORNIA

English translation © 1994 by B.A. Reichenbach

All rights reserved.

For permission to quote or excerpt, write to:

THE KOBER PRESS
P.O. Box 2194
San Francisco, California 94126-2194

This book is a translation from the German of *Das Buch vom Glück* by Bô Yin Râ, first published in 1920. The copyright to the German original is held by Kober Verlag AG, Bern, Switzerland.

Printed in the United States of America

Library of Congress Catalog Card Number: 94-077130

International Standard Book Number: 0-915034-04-02

Book design by Hal Hershey

Book cover after a design by Bô Yin Râ

THIS TRANSLATION IS
GRATEFULLY DEDICATED
TO
RUTH NIVOLA

CONTENTS

CONTENTS

PRELUDE

D ID YOU EVER watch a child create a castle in the sand and see it happily express its satisfaction when its work had been completed?

A LL OF YOU that seek true happiness in life can learn a lesson from this child.

For here you see a human being that has found its happiness, and if you will not seek to find your own, the same way as that child, you shall forever hunger after happiness in vain.

All happiness this mortal life affords—and only it shall be the topic of the present book— is joy experienced through creative effort. Be it that a person will create the timeless realm of love within his soul; be it that his creativity express itself within the province of the mind; or that material things provide his will the means creatively to manifest its power.

The joy experienced in creative work alone is real happiness, and all things else you might regard as such will surely, if you trust them, betray and rob you of true happiness, as much as one can find it in this life.

You ARE IN LOVE and in your love experience all the happiness you ever seek to know on earth? Tell me, what is your love, if not the joy you feel in what you are creating?

Emotions are the elements you have to work with in yourself; and if your love has truly brought you happiness, then you have built yourself a temple in the kingdom of your soul: a sanctuary only you can enter, and where you have enshrined the image of the deity you worship and would gladly serve.

Perhaps you never recognized that here is something of your own creation. Instead, you may have felt that you were being mastered by emotions, often led by them against your will; or you believed that you were held in chains, but such as you were glad to bear. And thus you thought all this was only forced upon you from outside and simply dealt with you according to eternal laws inherently connected with this life on earth.

However, you obstruct your own enlightenment if that is what you think.

To be sure, you merely bow to cosmic law, eternally invincible, when love imbues your soul with its dynamic energy, whose currents radiate throughout the universe and in mysterious ways cause human souls and bodies to become attracted to each other. Yet your compliance with this law holds no more than a promise of true happiness; a promise you will never see fulfilled, however, unless your love is able to awaken the creative faculties that you possess.

The happiness you then enjoy is of your own

creation. You had to struggle with a chaos of emotions, and now will reap your labor's fruits: that peace and harmony within the soul which works its own perfection by offering its whole self to another.

Indeed, even that purely carnal pleasure, which those regard as "love" who have no higher aspirations than to gratify their creature drives, becomes creative in a way; given that from lowest instincts it will cause their minds to build themselves a phantom shrine, wherein they elevate the idol of their sensual fantasies; but short-lived is the "happiness" that instinct offers to its slaves.

You, however, as a person seeking true and lasting happiness within your love will need to find a higher form of joy. And if your love is deep and pure, you shall not ever want to separate your physical sensations from the inner joy of souls whose essence is becoming one.

You never shall attain that happiness, however, unless you first create it.

You STILL ARE easily deceived and every day expect that "happiness" may somehow come your way from life outside.

Some believe they would be happy if they could only gain the love of just the person they adore; others, if they could achieve a certain goal; while not a few seek nothing more than being free of constant worries about their daily needs and wants.

But even should you have acquired all these things, you never can escape admitting to yourself that, in the end, there still is something lacking in your life and that your happiness is not complete. And so your restless search continues where you had once believed your goal would be achieved.

You cannot fathom what abundant joy this mortal life affords, nor do you realize that happiness which is created here on earth is both the ground and basis for every happiness in life beyond.

Your life on earth will have no meaning, but simply be a chain of never ending trials, more or less tormenting, relentlessly repeated every day—unless within your present life you find the happiness that physical existence offers you.

Do not believe the woeful doctrines that promise you unending bliss—in some "eternal" life—if you renounce the happiness you could enjoy on earth.

Bear in mind that even *here and now*—indeed, while you are reading this—you find yourself already in the very midst of your eternal life. And what you cannot here and now accomplish for yourself, no "God above" shall in your place create for you in all eternity.

You need to understand that happiness as such, quite independent of its form, is merely the result of using a capacity that you possess; and, further, that you never shall be truly happy, neither in this present, nor any future form of life, if you will not develop this capacity, but rather sit and idly wait till happiness might some day come your way; or, even worse, if you presume it ought to be awarded you in recognition of your worthy deeds, simply as a matter of God's justice.

Only by developing your own creative faculty shall you not merely find your happiness, but make it everlasting.

Only that which you yourself bring forth within you, here and now, will grant you timeless satisfaction.

Only if you can yourself create the kind of happiness you seek shall you possess enduring happiness in this and any other form of life.

CREATING HAPPINESS AS MORAL DUTY

CHAPTER ONE

CREATING HAPPINESS
AS MORAL DUTY

FEW HAVE THE GIFT of making happiness attend them all their days, and those few would do well to keep their secret to themselves; lest envy be aroused and slowly undermine the vigor of their lives.

Countless, on the other hand, are those who long for happiness with heart and soul, but cannot ever find it: because they do not know that happiness is something only they themselves are able to create.

They would pluck happiness like a forbidden fruit, hoping to obtain it at no cost, although they vaguely sense that one can have it only at a certain price.

From childhood on they heard it said that any

happiness on earth is but a gift of fickle chance, and that it was unworthy of a noble mind to strive for something so capricious.

They never heard of any teaching telling them about their obligation to use this life on earth in such a way that it becomes a source of constant joy.

Everyone, of course, desires to be "happy" and each attempts it in a different way. Still, finding happiness is looked upon as something incidental, a mere "bonus," and many other things are seen as more important than pursuing it above all else.

But those who would attain enduring happiness must make this end their highest goal. Whatever else they might desire to accomplish must be subordinated to, and wisely integrated with, that principal pursuit.

No other wish must interfere with their resolve to realize, by actions of their own free will, the highest form of happiness that life on earth may grant them.

No other task must they consider more important than their duty to attain the purest form of lasting happiness and, thereby, to increase its total store on earth, both for themselves and for mankind.

A GLOOMY DOCTRINE has since ancient times been spreading the belief that happiness on earth can only be attained by few, while all the rest of mankind has no hope of ever coming to enjoy it.

The world at large still does not know of the unlimited potential for both happiness and misery contained in life on earth; nor does it recognize that only human will—not merely wishful thinking—brings about what must occur.

Some feel sure their will is strong, but are in fact mere thralls of hopes and wishes, which may at times engage a fraction of their will. What they accomplish thus, however, already satisfies their modest expectation, and so they never aim for higher things, assuming to have reached the limits of what their will is able to achieve.

If mankind realized what human will has truly power to effect, one soon would find far greater numbers of happy souls on earth than even the most daring visionary could imagine, who dreams that any happiness on earth depends upon the victory of the utopian fancies with which he thinks he can improve the world.

WE ARE WHAT we resolve to be.

Fortune's whims shall only play with us as long as we permit blind fate to treat us as mere toys.

Misfortune shall be dogging all our steps as long as we keep running from it, in the hope that ill events might be escaped.

We shall remain the dispossessed of happiness as long as we refuse to recognize that it is our duty to create within this present life the highest form of happiness that each of us is able to achieve on earth.

Lacking the desire to be happy is a sin; a greater sin, however, is the lack of will to forge one's happiness in life on earth.

Sinful, too, and blasphemous before the Spirit's all-sustaining power is the wretched modesty that many show in their idea of happiness.

Some cannot imagine greater happiness than merely being able to feed and clothe their family without continual worry.

Others think the greatest happiness would be to live in royal castles and to travel in a golden coach.

Still others mean to find it by seeking fame and honors, high positions and renown.

Few seem to comprehend that neither wealth nor honors can ever make a person truly happy, but that in happiness resides a force that will provide, of all the treasures of this earth, to every individual precisely what he needs to lead a happy life—no more, no less.

Whoever thinks that happiness consists in

gaining hold of certain things in life is seeking still to gain those things; he is not striving after happiness.

Happiness is the contentment that creative will enjoys in its creation.

Yet this "creation" knows no end, and its creator's days of rest are merely Sabbaths of the soul, which will restore his energy for new creative work.

Whoever has found happiness is active without ceasing and never tires of employing his creative gifts.

What his activity creates is the prerequisite, the basis for his happiness. That happiness as such, however, is the force commanded by creative will, which of itself attracts all things that grant a person lasting satisfaction.

Not everyone will need the same, but all who undertake creating their own happiness are certain to attain whatever they require to achieve that end.

"SEEK YE FIRST the kingdom of God, and its righteousness; all other things shall then be added unto you."

How thoroughly they misinterpreted this saying of the Master of Nazareth.

Admittedly, he also said—according to the texts that have preserved his teachings—"the kingdom of God is not in this place, nor in that; it is in you." He thus quite clearly drew attention to an inner force in human beings the "righteousness"—the innate laws—of which must be obeyed before "all other things" can in effect be added. Yet who was ever bold enough to give those words the meaning the Master wanted to convey, expressing wisdom in the simplest form?

The "kingdom of God" he spoke about was meekly changed by minds of little faith into a realm of unctuous piety and feeble promises of future bliss. Or else they sought that kingdom in some distant world above, ignoring his own words which clearly stated that "the kingdom of heaven is at hand."

How very sad that human beings are so blinded by the veils of physical perception that they no longer sense how God's eternal kingdom can manifest itself within their soul, and that this kingdom is alive around them everywhere, no matter where they are, even if they thought they lived in "hell."

Human beings need merely seek their inner world, and there would find a treasure that eternities will not exhaust. They only need to send, into the world without, the currents of those energies which they command within—and all the earth would be renewed.

However, it has always been disclosed to all who through the ages were endowed with timeless knowledge that only few within this present aeon are prepared to let this will to free themselves become effective in their soul; and that a new age first must dawn, a new earth come into existence, before the "earnest waiting of the creature" for the "children of God" who will redeem the "whole creation, which is groaning and travailing in pain," such as St. Paul envisioned it, may finally become a cosmic fact.

The will of most is still too closely fettered, held under the hypnotic spell of physical perception, which in effect they cast themselves, and so they lack the courage to direct events of physical reality by virtue of the Spirit's power.

Devoid of faith they wait for some external thing that of itself might bring them help, without their own involvement; or else they have already buried all their hopes and expectations. Scarcely any can be found who even dare attempt to make themselves the spiritual rulers of their own existence.

Yet even in this present age those few might grow in number. Indeed, there are already some who vaguely sense a power they possess within, although they do not know how one may learn to master it.

The insights offered in the present book will guide them in the right direction. Its author merely gave expression to what since ancient times had always been kept secret, disclosed to very few by those appointed to protect it.

It is knowledge firmly rooted in experience, tried and proven through the ages, and none who put it to the test has ever found it wanting.

Those who now convey this knowledge have decided to disclose it to the world at large, and to accept responsibility for that decision.

THE SECRET TRUTH behind all happiness in life on earth is like a seamless ring.

Within yourself alone you find the power to create your happiness, and every form of happiness is rooted wholly in the use of that creative force; for only the contentment which this force imparts is true and lasting happiness.

It is your given duty to put that unawakened force in you to active use. It is your duty to create whatever be the highest form of happiness

attainable to you on earth. And how you best
may here fulfill that given task the present
book will tell you.

CHAPTER TWO

"I" AND "YOU"

WHEN YOU SAY "I" your consciousness embraces only your own self, and in that conscious "I" you have no room for any other.

You are, for your own self, the very center of the world.

For your own self you are the conscious self of all mankind.

However, this mankind is a totality of homogeneous elements, and it comprises billions of distinctive "selves." While not a single one of these will be exactly like your own, nonetheless, according to their inner structure, they all are perfectly identical with that which in yourself you feel as being "I".

It is not easy to convey through language

what here I wish to make you comprehend, and so I have to ask you intuitively to discern the meaning of my words; for well I know that total clarity can in this matter not be gained through speech. And furthermore, I only can express myself in my own way, which you may have to "translate" first into your way of thinking.

I want to make you realize that you are the uniquely structured "center" of an integrated organism which is composed of only such distinctive "centers." But since this organism is in essence infinite, although not without limits, it has its proper "center" in each of its constituent parts.

Each individuated center, however, perceives itself as "I", and all the other similar centers it regards as "You."

If, as a center of that organism, you would create your individual happiness, you need to keep that fact in mind, and must endeavor to discover the relationships that secretly prevail between each living "I" and "You."

These relationships are constantly in flux, however, and need to be considered differently every moment.

One thing alone remains immutably established: the strictly regulated way in which the consequences of all actions and reactions are permanently kept in balance within the life of mankind as a whole.

The individuated self you are can influence another self in no more than two ways; that is, either unintentionally, without your seeking some effect, or on purpose, in order to achieve a certain end.

If it is your will to influence some other self, however, the means at your disposal are: requests, persuasion, or the use of force.

Bear in mind, however, that you shall have to pay a fixed, inexorable price for all the consequences of your deeds; in fact, for even actions that you merely contemplate.

You thus should not persuade nor beg another if you yourself will not be moved by pleas and by persuasion. But most of all, do not resort to force if you consider any force against your person to be intolerable violence.

You will not get away with anything you do, no matter how secure you think you are, or how well hidden you might deem your true intentions.

No doubt, you can conceal your aims from any fellow self, but to the integrated organism of mankind as a whole, every impulse of your being is instantly disclosed. And sooner or later, at a time determined by inherent laws, you will, by inescapable necessity, confront the consequences of your actions.

If you are deaf to all requests, yet make appeals to others; if no one can persuade you, while you rely upon persuasion; if you object to being forced, but do not shrink from using force against another: you will in each such case achieve results for which perhaps you think you did not have to pay the price. But here you are mistaken!

The Spirit's laws cannot, like human rules, be cleverly evaded, nor bent to your advantage; and nowhere shall you find an advocate who might attempt to save you from the consequences of your deeds.

You shall be forced to pay in full all debts you owe mankind, resulting from your conduct toward any human being; nor, indeed, shall you escape the Spirit's law until you paid "the uttermost farthing."

The longer the extension you are granted to repay your debts, the more acutely should you be concerned; because your liabilities—with interest both simple and compounded—shall not be waived in all eternity.

But even that is still not all.

For you may well incur indebtedness to mankind even for yourself, because you likewise are accountable for your own person. And thus you should not make demands upon yourself for which you have no hope of gaining compensation from mankind.

Otherwise, you sooner or later will be forced to pay the price, with interest compounded, for all indebtedness toward your own self, exactly as you would for any other person.

Pᴇʀʜᴀᴘꜱ ᴛʜɪꜱ ɪꜱ the first time you have heard of this inexorable law? Or you have only now begun to recognize its logical effectiveness and unforgiving justice?

Perhaps you feel concerns arising in your mind because of things you may have done, although you are determined in future carefully to weigh your actions according to that law?

Iꜰ ʏᴏᴜ ᴀʀᴇ ᴡɪʟʟɪɴɢ to create your happiness in life, you shall no doubt discover ways to pay your debts to mankind in a form of your own choosing, once you have in fact determined how much you actually still owe.

You need not wait until the Spirit's law presents its claims, with merciless indifference as to your weal and woe.

Draw up a "balance sheet" of your existence, and do not be alarmed if what you owe is vastly in excess of what you own.

Although the organism constituting mankind as a whole must ruthlessly collect, from every single member, all debts they "inadvertently" had failed to pay, that organism is no less indifferent and automatic in following another law: one that strictly bars it from forcefully collecting any payment the moment you are earnestly resolved to settle your accounts in full, and shall continue to acknowledge your indebtedness. And this resolve will shield you even if your present circumstances may not permit you to repay your total debts at once without creating new indebtedness, and thereby causing further damage, either to yourself or others.

If you would find enduring happiness, you need to know at least as much as I have outlined here about the law of compensation governing the organism formed by mankind as a whole.

You may, if you desire, further trace the manifold effects and consequences of this law in daily human life. Indeed, you well might find that quite instructive.

In seeking to create your happiness in life you soon may recognize that possibly the largest part of your envisioned happiness is closely interwoven with the many-faceted relationships affecting life between yourself and all the other "selves" that you may find around you.

The happiness you seek would also comprehend the realm of love in all its forms.

Yet love—and I do not mean only sexual union—always needs an "opposite," even if that "opposite" should be yourself.

Here, too, your life is subject to the law of compensation, and thus you ought not to expect your love to be secure from disappointment if you complacently neglect to do your share, or would receive more than you give.

For anything you want to have you needs

must offer full equivalents; otherwise, the organism constituting mankind as a whole shall one day claim from you what you have failed to give. You then should not complain, however, if it exacts its due by means not in the least affected by your wishes.

Whether it concerns the way you deal with total strangers, or the affection that you feel and seek to gain in a relationship connecting man and woman; whether it concerns the love of parents for their children, that of children for their parents, or of siblings toward each other: you ought not to expect that you can rightfully receive more than you give. And should that case arise, see to it that you promptly offer something in return; lest what you owe should one day be demanded from you when you least expect it, and in ways you may find thoroughly unpleasant.

THE LAWS THAT regulate the Spirit's life are no less automatic and immutable than are the laws of physics that govern matter in external life. Now if you disregard a law of nature, you know from personal experience that you must bear the consequences, whether it please you or not.

It would be equally presumptuous of you to seek "forgiveness"—that is to say: exemption from all consequences—after violating spiritual law as it would be when breaking any law of nature. In either case you would be asking that the order of the universe be cast aside because of your transgression.

Since human beings do commit such errors daily in the billions, any such "forgiveness" would be tantamount to plunging all the worlds of Spirit into chaos and eternal night.

WAKE UP AND shake from you the gloomy superstition of the savage who will quarrel with his fetish when it seems to disobey his will. Instead, create within yourself an active faith in the immeasurable greatness of the spiritual body of which you are a part and, thus, an individuated center. Perhaps you

then will realize how abject is your concept
of a Godhead of which you dare expect that
it should set your foolish whims above its
own established order any time you do not
wish to face the consequences that your actions have upon the spiritual organism of
which you are a part.

If one day you acquire final knowledge, you
shall with deepest shame look back upon the
days when you believed it quite in order that
"God's own son" should suffer for your
"sins," because you found this a convenient
way to rid yourself of any consequences of
your deeds.

That day you shall no longer comprehend
how you could not have rather craved annihi-
lation of your very being than bear the
thought for even a moment that an innocent
should suffer death and torture to pay for
your transgressions.

But though you may be someone who feels
responsible for every deed, I fear you may

not know as yet that you are equally accountable for each and every thought.

As I already told you, nothing can be hidden from mankind's spiritual body of which you are a part. Indeed, that body is aware of even your most secret thoughts.

Yet here you should not form the wrong idea, as if I meant to say that there exists a common, or "collective soul" of mankind, as if it were a conscious, independent being in itself.

It is only through its individuated human centers that the organism constituting mankind as a whole is capable of being conscious. And in each particular center it is conscious differently, aware of its existence in varying degrees of clarity.

If I assert that nothing ever can be hidden from mankind's spiritual organism, I would merely have you recognize that everything you do or think will automatically, and far beyond your person, influence and have effects upon that organism as a whole. You thus may later often search in vain for causes to account for such effects, because you never dreamed that even your most secret thoughts, which you felt hidden almost from yourself, could be the source of such far-reaching consequences.

If you are to become the purposeful creator of your happiness, you must remember that your thoughts will serve you well—as faithful beasts of burden—provided you have trained them for that task. But they will turn into unbridled forces of destruction if you allow them to throw off their yoke and let them roam at will.

You cannot find true happiness if you will not, as far as you are able, help other people to create their own. But you destroy their happiness if your own thoughts behave like savage boars that trample on the flower beds of other souls.

If harmonies inform your thoughts you shall inspire harmonies in others; but if your thoughts are bent on chaos and destruction, it will be chaos and destruction you arouse in them.

You cannot properly maintain your health without consistent thoughts embracing beauty, strength, and soundness. On the other hand, your thoughts will cause you to become a seedbed of contagion if, wallowing in your infirmities, your mind is occupied by only sickness and disease.

Someone that I know had been pronounced "incurable" by his physicians, and his disease was of a kind for which the medical profession has still not found a cure. Yet, by the power of his thoughts he cured himself, and has for decades since enjoyed a healthy life.

I also know another, who was informed, at his insistence, that he would only live another four or five years at the most. He neither used the remedies prescribed by his physicians, nor followed any special regimen. Instead, he set himself the goal to stay alive by virtue only of his mental strength. Twenty years have passed since he was given up, yet he is still alive, both vigorous and healthy, without a trace of illness. And now he hardly can believe that he had ever needed a physician.

Such people are like focal points reflecting health and vigor, and their example touches others near and far, even if, judging strictly by medical standards, they cannot be considered truly "cured."

They simply feel they have recovered, and time has shown that to be true; for their complaints have disappeared.

The confidence they gained through their success now gives their mental strength invincible effectiveness, and thus they serve as fountains of good health for others, even from afar.

LET YOUR THOUGHTS be constantly immersed in poverty and want, and want and poverty shall not be long in finding you. Continuously harbor fears of some misfortune, and disasters shall not fail to dog your steps.

Refuse, however, to regard your cause as lost, even in the darkest hour, and you shall never be defeated. You soon will find a way to deal with your predicament.

Treat any mishap you encounter as you would a thunderstorm that caught you at a picnic, and you may rest assured that mishaps shall befall you less and less.

You ARE YOURSELF the magnet for your fortune, whether it be good or bad.

You can "attune" your being to the energies you would attract, and they must then obey your will.

Your actions as an individuated self do not affect yourself alone, however, but also every other self that is connected with you, in a spiritual way, within the organism constituting mankind as a whole.

The degree of your effectiveness will be determined far less than you think by factors of external distance. Instead, all levels of intensity depend upon the relative degree of similarity between your own unique "vibrations" and those of other human selves. Still, each among the billions whom you regard as "others" will somehow, in some manner, be affected by the final consequences of events that you have set in motion.

Thus it follows that you bear immense responsibility!

You never truly are alone, all by yourself, even when you think that you are safely hidden behind the thickest walls.

Even as a single, individuated self you only act in concert and connection with all other selves; for while each human being is a unique identity, all individuated "centers" within the organism constituting mankind as a whole are, in the end, of only one identity.

CHAPTER THREE

LOVE

ANY DISCUSSION OF human happiness must of necessity include the special kind two human beings can create for one another by their love.

One easily forgets, however, that happiness within the realm of love, as in all other forms, needs first to be created.

Many people live their lives from year to year in constant expectation that happiness will some day cross their path; and not a few among them seek no other form of happiness than that which man and woman find in mutual love.

Some wait in vain throughout their lives, because the kind of happiness they dream about continues somehow to elude them.

Others some day come to feel that they have found their happiness in someone whom they love, yet before long their hopes are disappointed and they despair of ever being able to find happiness in love that will endure.

Foolish talk about a natural "antagonism" supposedly at work between the sexes now finds willing ears and thus completes the damage.

Yet those who are in this way "dis-illusioned" are actually still far from being truly rid of their deception; indeed, they merely substitute one error for another.

At first they had believed that happiness attained in love is no more than a gift of chance, a present one may find and then shall own forever, all without one's doing.

They now seem free of that conceit, but only in regard to their respective choice of partner. And thus they instantly fall victim to the next deception, by assuming that their past unhappiness was merely the result of their poor choice.

How VERY SAD! And yet, how wrong! Truly, those of you who feel they have been cheated of the happiness they sought in love may rest assured that the initial impulse which had drawn you to each other was clearly, in most cases, no mistake. You now deceive yourselves, however, because you cannot rid your minds of the assumption that happiness through love is found without some effort on your part.

You still are unaware that you must first create the happiness you would enjoy, if it is ever to become your permanent possession, an enrichment of your lives which you can never lose.

Your will to realize enduring happiness was still not unencumbered.

You doubtless had the wish to savor all the happiness that love may bring—yet wishes never have commanding force. The power of your will, however, which alone could have created that enduring joy, this energy you dissipated by your striving after countless little things, instead of gathering its forces to achieve one single goal: creating your own happiness.

THOSE WHO DO NOT merely wish, but truly want to find their happiness through love must concentrate and aim their will at only that specific goal, and not at anything besides.

They should not take for granted what they must first create. They should not seek to eat the fruit before it grew and ripened, as dreamers do in sleep. For they would sorely miss that fruit if suddenly reality were to assert itself and rudely woke them from their dreams.

From the very day their love awakens they must set out to develop, in themselves, a constant will to make their happiness reality. And to that single will must they subordinate all things their wishes may desire.

HAPPINESS WITHIN the realm of love can only be achieved if one is singlemindedly, indeed tenaciously resolved to find enduring joy with just the person whom one loves.

Not even for a moment must one play with the idea that things might not perhaps "work out."

Happiness in the domain of love—as in all other spheres of life—is joy created by one's proper action. It is the pleasure one is granted by any work well done. It is at once that work itself, and also the capacity to bring that work about.

In the domain of love, however, this work consists in making the beloved person happy through our actions. The happiness that we in turn enjoy is then the satisfaction of knowing that we indeed possess the power to achieve that goal.

But one that holds the power to make a person happy, likewise has the power of causing him profoundest grief.

Unless your will resolves each day anew to use the power that you have exclusively for bringing happiness into the life of your beloved, that power will fall prey to hosts of demons— all those desires, great and small, which daily life induces every hour.

Then, if your love is real, it may perhaps not die completely, despite incessantly repeated grief. The happiness you sought in love, however, and which in days of celebrating, merriment, and wishful thinking you may have thought you had already found, that happiness will soon abandon you and not become a treasure you possess.

You then may ask yourselves, Why is it that we cannot understand each other? Why do we constantly bring misery into each other's life, even though within our hearts we feel that our love for one another is sincere, despite the torment that we cause each other?

But thus you shall not find the answer that alone can bring you peace. Instead, you keep renewing promises and pledges to each other in days when all is well, only to ignore and break them just as promptly. And so you slowly wear each other down and in the end resign yourselves at best to lead a tolerable coexistence, convinced of simply being victims of some cruel fate.

However, in most cases this is only self-deception, caused by the delusion that happiness can be conceived in dreams, and met with as imagined if one but hopes and wishes—instead of being a possession our will must truly want, and then determines to create.

Still, even now you have not altogether lost the happiness you once desired, if in your heart is yet alive a trace of true affection for each other. But first you need to recognize that what prevented you from finding happiness in love was merely that you thought you could enjoy what you had not yourself created. In other words, you meant to harvest without having sown.

This very day, however, can you begin to learn how one may truly live a life imbued with love. This very day you can wake up and end the dream that brought you only sacrifice and painful disappointment.

No DOUBT THERE WILL BE many things that you must now forgive each other, things perhaps not easy to forgive, and many an angry word will long remain etched deeply in your soul. Yet if there ever was true love between you, even for a day, you soon shall clearly see that you had in effect deceived yourselves, and that whatever you must now forgive each other had once been only hurled against a phantom, shaped in anger by your mind; a phantom you thought real and likely think so even now, because it had become the image whose very form the one you love then actually assumed.

Above ALL ELSE you now must earnestly resolve to see each other in a different light, if you would have your ailing love recover and are determined to create the kind of happiness you want; a happiness not prone to disappointment.

At first you may not find it easy to control your deep suspicion which, like a fixed idea, is ever searching to discover whether possibly the once beloved, whom long ago you almost learned to hate, does not still only see the phantom image of yourself, which is deluding heart and mind.

Yet if, in spite of all initial setbacks and relapses, you daily shall renew your single-minded will to exercise whatever power over one another you may hold exclusively to make each other truly happy, you soon will learn how to create the happiness you seek.

PERHAPS YOU NOW will say, "What is achieved though I act with the best intention to make our marriage happy, but if my partner lacks the same resolve?"

As long as such a question can distract your mind you have not fully grasped the meaning of "creating one's own happiness."

You still would like to see yourself dependent on external things, because you lack the courage to take control of your own life.

You still have little confidence in your own self and are a long way yet from truly wanting to employ your will.

Once you have in truth resolved to find your happiness in marriage you must no longer even feel it matters whether your intention is supported by your spouse or not.

You must completely silence all your wishes, so that they can no longer interfere with the direction of your will.

All your resolve must be directed toward a single goal: successfully to use the power you possess to make the one you love profoundly happy.

Enjoying your success will then become a source of happiness for you.

To be successful in one's efforts, one here must learn to practice much self-discipline.

You will have to inhibit inclinations, control your temper and your moods, and constantly must set aside your wishes. All this, however, you shall find a source of joy and satisfaction; for you shall come to know what happiness you can already gain by merely being master in yourself in situations where today you may not even realize how thoroughly you still are shackled by so much that is not even your own self.

Perhaps you now still get upset when seeing that the one you love holds wrong ideas on matters that you judge correctly; or tends to like things you detest, and that your views in matters of "good taste" are often far apart.

Of what significance are all those things, however, when weighed against the joy one finds in love?

How trivial and irrelevant compared to all the happiness two human souls can offer one another through their love!

Whichever of you might be right or wrong in any situation is altogether unimportant where the only thing that matters is to build a sound foundation for the happiness you want to find in love.

It merely is an abject craving for a substitute of real power if you insist your spouse should automatically adopt your way of seeing things in life; nor does it matter whether your ideas are right in fact, or only in your mind, and thus may well be altogether wrong.

Once you begin to see that your ability to make the other person happy proves to be effective, you will be quite astonished to discover that both your ways of seeing things, which earlier had often been in conflict, have suddenly been reconciled.

With some embarrassment you then must grant that all your former arguments about some trivial issue, which at the time had seemed of great importance, were actually quite foolish.

You then will understand that you could not succeed in unifying your conflicting views before you had found harmony within your individual selves.

THE HAPPINESS THAT love imparts must be created before it can bring forth that twofold unity which shall defy all separation and division, and make you one in all your thoughts and feelings.

In your love, my friends, as in all other things, you have a moral duty to create enduring happiness; and all your disappointments are rooted only in your failure to fulfill that obligation.

CHAPTER FOUR

WEALTH AND POVERTY

ALL LIFE WITHIN the universe is the effect of polar opposites: reciprocal exchange of energies between opposed polarities.

Whoever would get rid of wealth in order to abolish poverty has still not understood that also wealth and poverty depend upon each other, since every pole demands its counterpart.

Only when related poles remain in undiminished opposition can life arise and find its form; and only then will also human effort flourish and succeed.

Wherever polar opposition is abolished, things are ruined and destroyed.

Whoever truly wants to help the poor must

rather seek to increase wealth. Yet neither wealth nor poverty need of necessity for all time show the gross and brutal deformations which until now are still the only forms that mankind seems to know.

There is truth in saying: "Blessed are the poor"; yet being poor must not mean destitution.

Wealth can vouchsafe blessings without measure; but then it must not, gorged and unproductive, only wallow in that vulgar depth concerning which a godly teacher once remarked that sooner would "a camel go through the eye of a needle, than a rich man enter the kingdom of God."

Since ancient times a false belief has kept alive the notion that the resources of this planet were not only very scarce, but could not be sufficiently increased to guarantee that no one living on this earth would have to suffer want. And thus arose a concept of the wealthy which understandably had to embitter many who still lived in dire need.

One would be closer to the truth if it were recognized that, while it cannot be excused if even one among the millions living on this earth were forced to suffer want, the wealth that some enjoy is not in any way the cause that might explain why others live in poverty.

It is an absolute and fundamental duty of mankind to guarantee that none of its members is deprived of life's necessities; to provide that every human being, however one might judge the person's value or importance, have shelter, food, and clothing. And this responsibility extends no less to individuals who make no contribution whatsoever to society.

If a person prove destructive, he may be isolated and confined. One has no right, however, to withhold the basic needs of life from even such an individual. Nor is one justified in keeping from him the resources that are needed should he seek to raise his inner being from the depth to which he fell.

WHAT NOWADAYS is seen as "punishment" of criminals is but a wretched undertaking;

because it is not guided by the recognition that all of mankind is a closely interwoven organism and that, consequently, all of mankind bears responsibility for any crimes that are committed and which it proved unable to contain.

More enlightened knowledge shall here in future do much better; namely, by preventing crime as such. Today, by contrast, it is still considered almost as a law of nature, and one is chiefly bent on "punishing the criminal."

But even disregarding "criminals," there always will be individuals whose usefulness for mankind's physical well-being may not be very obvious, but who must nonetheless be kept secure from want, if mankind as a whole is not to harm itself through their condition.

That much one ought to bear in mind concerning want, which mankind must endeavor to abolish lest it should cause damage to its organism as a whole, and thus inflict still further harm upon itself.

But never should society attempt to do away with wealth and poverty as such, if it would not in fact destroy itself.

Wealth and poverty are polar opposites that are essential for sustaining mankind's life on earth; because it is precisely their polarity that causes the dynamic tension which mankind's total organism needs if one day it is truly to fulfill its cosmic task.

Doomed is a society where wealth no longer can be honored and respected.

But doomed alike is one that will no longer honor and respect its poor.

HONORABLE, TRULY, are the poor who bear their indigence with dignity; but no less worthy to be honored are the rich who treat the burden of their wealth as but a loan for which they are accountable to mankind as a whole.

Let neither side disdain the other! Indeed, both rich and poor should recognize that each is of the same importance for the whole.

It would be wrong, however, to assume that poverty, which mankind needs no less than wealth, must of necessity be always close to destitution in order to provide the polar opposite to wealth.

Both wealth and poverty are concepts whose significance is purely relative.

The higher the level of wealth, the higher, too, will rise the upper line of poverty; and there can be, in contrast to substantial wealth, a form of poverty which may itself, among the poor, be looked upon as riches.

You are a part and individuated center of mankind's organism as a whole, and thus you always have the right to strive for all the wealth this planet has to offer you.

How much of it you can in fact acquire depends upon your "karma": your inborn capability of ruling your own fate.

Nonetheless, you always should endeavor to attain the highest relative degree of wealth that, in your own best judgment, appears accessible to you by honest means.

You must not think that by decreasing the number of the poor you might disturb the tension that polarity demands.

Even if the number of the rich on earth should be increased a thousandfold, all poverty would still not disappear. Indeed, if all the world's inhabitants were somehow to grow wealthy, the difference between their riches would yet remain so great that true polarity would always be preserved.

The earth is so immeasurably rich in ways of being wealthy that such a state of things is not impossible. In our day, however, it is not to be expected; for the majority of people still do not know about the spiritual laws that regulate the ways by which the earth bestows its treasures. And even if these laws were widely known, few only would be willing to comply with rules where they, instead, prefer to get things free, not hampered by restrictions.

Here, too, obtains above all else the law of compensation, of interchange and balance, and thus you never will be able to receive and to retain a value for which you did not pay the proper price; for which, in other words, you are not willing to exchange equivalents of fully corresponding worth.

Now and then, perhaps, you may be given things without such compensation, and you might then believe they will be yours to keep. However, you shall very soon have lost them, no matter how you try to safeguard your possession.

What I have outlined here is governed by the most inexorable laws, which are no less impossible to circumvent than those that rule the energies of matter in the realm of physical reality.

You have a right to all the riches you desire; and yet, for even the most modest form of wealth you must consent to offer fully corresponding value.

You may point out that there are people who possess their riches through inheritance; however, that is not in conflict with the law discussed above.

For, clearly, someone had at one time offered such equivalents; and if the heir should not consistently provide sufficient further compensation, he one day surely will have lost the wealth that others had created.

This, however, may take time and only happen to that heir's descendants; for spiritual laws will always strictly function according to the impulse that had striven to comply with their demands.

A fortune rapidly amassed shall also vanish just as quickly, unless new impulses endeavor to protect it. On the other hand, possessions that a lifetime built with patient toil will long be held together, even if the heirs should clearly not prove worthy.

Only you must never think that there is some injustice in the way these laws effect events.

Nor, for that matter, are you thereby deprived of anything.

It always is within your power to achieve whatever your ability allows you to achieve; and your ability will let you gain the things your will pursues in earnest.

In striving thus you must not let it trouble you that others seem to have great wealth which they did not themselves create.

The earth possesses such enormous wealth that it will always have at hand, even for you, the most immense of fortunes.

However, you must not mistake your wishes for your will!

Your wishes may become effective only if they should succeed in rallying your will behind them.

Strong-willed individuals are known to have created fortunes of immeasurable worth, even where they had to start in dire poverty. Dreamers, on the other hand, who are content with wishful thinking, can be found on every street. But rarely will you see that one of them is able to command sufficient will to realize a fraction even of his dreams.

IF THEN YOU WOULD attain the wealth that you are able to create, you must above all else beware of feeling any sense of envy.

Given that one day you would yourself be seen as rich—although it merely were among the poor—you must regard each wealthy person you encounter as a pledge: a promise giving you assurance that also you are able to attain your goal.

You must find satisfaction in the knowledge that there are wealthy people in the world. Indeed, you ought to see their riches as a precondition, so to speak, of the fulfillment of your own intent and will.

Again, if you desire to grow rich, do not become a penny-pinching miser.

You doubtless will find many rich who are quite careful with their money; but you would search in vain to show me even one among the truly rich who gained his wealth by only watching pennies.

If, then, you are determined to grow wealthy, and if you think that riches are essential for your happiness, be sure to search your heart and soul for the equivalents that you intend to offer in return for any wealth you hope to gain.

Neither here on earth, nor in eternal life will you at any time be given things for free; and if it happens that you must accept a gift, even of the kind that one exchanges on certain festive occasions, you ought to ask yourself at once how you might best give mankind something in return; for you will otherwise be made to pay for it by means you may not like.

As you have seen, it is not all that easy to meet the various requirements you are expected to fulfill if you indeed mean to acquire even very modest wealth.

But rest assured, no mortal ever came by wealth in any other way, even if he could not consciously account for all his actions.

Values of all kinds are constantly exchanged in life on earth.

There is nothing that you can acquire and possess for long if you will not give something that has equal value in exchange.

On the other hand, if you have nothing you can offer, you should in justice not presume you are entitled to receive.

You never shall acquire worth beyond the price you pay.

Do not indulge in wishful thinking!

Wealth is governed by exacting laws, and only by exchange of values, which you possess within yourself, can you gain property of any kind.

CHAPTER FIVE

MONEY

MOST GENUINE idealists may well be shocked to see that in a book on spiritual values of the highest kind there suddenly is mention of so base a thing as "money."

That money functions as a medium expressing spiritual relationships and, thus, obeys the Spirit's laws, is probably the last thing they suspect.

Instead, they rather would not hear of money, nor of money matters, and I can understand that very well; for I myself consider all financial dealings among the least agreeable requirements we face in life on earth.

But here it mainly is the outer form which causes such aversion, while the object in itself

embodies spiritual nature in the highest degree.

No reader of daily stock exchange quotations
is likely to suspect that laws originating in the
Spirit, whose essence animates all matter, have
in those columns found their perfect and complete expression.

Most people of refined aesthetic inclinations
see money as a "dirty" thing, having passed
through many hands, and they are loath to
touch whatever smells of "filthy lucre" without gloves.

But all that notwithstanding, money truly is a
sacred thing. And I make bold to say this, although I know full well there will be self-
anointed saints who now shall see me as a
rank blasphemer.

To my regret, I cannot be of help to such ethe-
real dreamers. And, what is worse, I do suspect there will be those among them who,
while they may not consider money some-

thing "sacred," are not above desiring to secure it by any means whatever, fair or foul.

Money simply is the physical expression of the value which anything originating in the Spirit is able to attain in the domain of matter.

Spiritual values, too, are ultimately property and wealth; for there are no possessions of whatever kind that one could not, in one form or another, trace back to things originating in the Spirit.

Yet readers of the present book who would create their own enduring happiness within this day and age will clearly not be able to avoid the use of money.

They must prepare themselves to see that money in effect is not at all the "evil" thing as which it is maligned by long tradition. Rather, they must learn to speak of it with some respect if they would know its true significance.

Let me repeat again: Money is a sacred thing;

for it expresses the intrinsic value which spiritual realities of any kind are able to secure within the realm of matter.

To be sure, most people think of money chiefly as a means to pay their bills. They do not realize that in this life one can—indeed, more often must—make payments in some other coin.

They do not know that money is an element that can express enduring spiritual values, and so they think it is profane to speak of it as representing spiritual qualities.

Nonetheless, there is no more compelling proof revealing the effective force of spiritual values within this world of matter than the one we know as money in its various forms.

All great values of the Spirit ever manifested on this planet have without exception caused substantial and far-reaching movements in the realm of money.

In order to gain recognition in this world, spiritual values have to, as it were, associate themselves with matter. They must themselves assume material form if they are to produce effects in the domain of matter.

There is no other way in which material life could ever even be informed of their existence.

No matter how sublime a spiritual value might appear, if it should fail to set in motion the universally accepted form expressing all material values, i.e., money, such a value will be lost and useless to mankind.

The more substantial the amounts of money set in motion by a given spiritual value, the more securely anchored it will be in the material world.

THERE IS A lesson to be learned from this.

Do not expect that you are able, for all of your "idealism," to benefit mankind in any way, or that your good intentions could prevail, as long as you treat money, and the value it embodies, with disdain.

Of course you should not kneel before and worship "Mammon," nor look upon "possessing" money as an end in itself. The goal of your endeavors should be, instead, its active circulation. The aim is, therefore, not so much possession, as rather the ability to set in motion ever larger sums of money in support of spiritual values.

However little money you might call your own, you always should remain aware that there is hidden power even in a penny. And as the smallest stone can start a massive avalanche, so may a penny trigger large-scale movements in the sphere of money.

But then you also must have faith in the dynamic force that manifests itself in money.

That hidden force reacts quite negatively to the slightest lack of faith. On the other hand, it never disappoints a trust that is unshakeable and fortified by patience.

The more money you have working for you in the service of a worthy cause, the more reliably will you be getting your investment back again with time, together with all interest that has accrued.

If, on the other hand, you meant to test your money's power with only paltry sums and feelings of distrust, you run the risk of losing even the little you so hesitantly ventured.

You should, of course, not irresponsibly take risks beyond your means, but always carefully consider whether the amounts required for some venture are in proportion to what you can afford. Otherwise you may discover that even the sublimest value of the Spirit, which you intended to establish in this world, may in the end for you become a curse and a disaster.

Any enterprise through which you offer something truly useful to mankind is certain to create an increase also in material values in due time. Still, every undertaking calls for the commensurate investment, and if the proper sums are not at your disposal, it is better that you not become involved at all; even if supporting such a venture seems to promise you substantial gains and could become a boon for all mankind.

Your aim would be dishonest from the start if you expected to reap profits although you were not able to contribute the required share of capital.

Nor should you ever operate with other people's money, pursuing goals you personally believe important, unless you can be certain that your sources have the means the enterprise requires, whereby they shall in time create new values, which then assure them of returns proportionate to their investment.

Lacking that assurance, you simply might be risking all your sources' wealth. And in that case, the Spirit's laws, which govern mankind as a whole, would then hold you alone responsible for all the damage you have caused.

THESE LAWS have ways of reaching every individual in one form or another, and ultimately shall collect their claims to the "uttermost farthing." Nor do they care about the currency in which you might be able to repay your debts, or that the people you had harmed shall thereby not gain any benefit.

The laws that spiritually govern mankind as a whole are never interested in compensating those who suffered damage, nor in punishing the author of such loss. Their only function is effectively to keep in balance the organically connected life of mankind as a whole. For them each individual can take the place of any other; and any person, even without knowing it, may thus become the instrument of their inexorable, automatically proceeding will.

In a higher sense, there is no real "ownership" of money.

The person seemingly possessing it is no more than the temporary guardian of a portion of the wealth that is collectively created in the world of matter by the activity of mankind as a whole.

The magnitude of wealth a person temporarily may "own," simply demonstrates his talent for serving as a "steward" of such values. And one who faithfully takes care of little things, and thereby generates new wealth, him shall the Spirit's laws, which regulate the organism comprising all mankind, with certainty appoint one day to govern also over many things; provided that his will, not merely wishful thinking, shall earnestly pursue that goal.

The recurring setbacks that so many seemingly quite capable individuals tend to experience are always proof that they in one way or another habitually offend against the rules of spiritual law, without suspecting their mistake.

Be it that their will lacks energy and is replaced by hopes and wishes, or that they only partially comply with certain aspects of these laws, while disregarding others.

Nor do many people realize that the extent to which they may create new wealth is not a matter they are able to decide. Instead, each sum employed must generate a fixed return of value, whether this amount be less or more than what had been desired.

Consequently, there are people who work diligently year after year, haunted by recurring failures, but unaware that somewhere they are gravely violating spiritual laws, of whose existence they had never heard.

HERE ONE MIGHT perhaps assume that I have only those in mind who, either with their own, or borrowed moneys, are engaged in enterprises they possess and personally control.

However, I am likewise thinking of the many thousands who are employed and work for someone else.

In their case, frequently entire categories have to suffer for the wrongs committed by a few. Here, then, each person's individual responsibility becomes immense indeed. On the other hand, wherever spiritual laws are heeded, the lives of countless human beings will be substantially improved.

FROM THE MOMENT you accept employment in the service of another, you take upon yourself complete responsibility for the specific sector of his enterprise that is entrusted to your care. As a result, all violations of the Spirit's laws of which you might be guilty will have the same effect for your existence as if you had been acting in your own behalf.

The best advice I have to give you, whether your position be regarded high or low, is to act at all times exactly as you would if you were to perform your given duties for yourself and for your personal benefit.

If you believe that you are "underpaid," you should endeavor to improve your compensation by pursuing the respective means you have available. Do not forget, however, that even the most insufficient pay will never free you from the obligation to think and act according to the spiritual laws one must obey in matters touching money; otherwise, it will be you who comes to grief because your conduct had created damage for another.

You also need to know that your remuneration always is determined very justly by the Spirit's law, precisely in proportion to your efforts and commitment. As a result, you one day must receive, down to the last penny, in one form or another, whatever your employer might have unjustly kept from you. On the other hand, if you were granted higher compensation than was justified by your engagement, interest, and effort, every penny you collected in excess shall one day be reclaimed from you without appeal or mercy.

In order to effect that constant state of balance, which spiritual laws must by necessity maintain, these laws treat every form of value as fully interchangeable equivalents. And so you may perhaps receive—or, for that matter, lose—in a completely different "currency" whatever is your rightful due, or what you, on the other hand, may have obtained unjustly.

Money is the agent representing all material values. Yet to secure the balance which spiritual laws are obligated to enforce, it does not matter whether they achieve that end by means of a particular value, or by the agent symbolizing all material values, namely money.

PERHAPS YOU NOW will understand why I referred to money as a "sacred" thing; given that it symbolizes every value that this earth bestows. In addition, it physically expresses anything of value created by the Spirit's influence on matter, for which it is at once the agent and the connecting link.

Whether you wish to or not, you will have to consider money among the tools to build your happiness on earth. And if you would successfully create that happiness, you will have to respect the hidden laws that recognize in money, and in all values that it represents, the active servant of the Spirit's will.

CHAPTER SIX

OPTIMISM

For those who are determined to create their own enduring happiness on earth there is no longer any pointless daily grind, nor any fear, or worry.

They feel an energy within themselves that triumphs over all things that seem threatening or dreary.

They will today not harbor anxious thoughts about the troubles of tomorrow, and yet each day they live will be the perfect preparation for the day to follow.

They shall discover how one learns the art of living in the present, and how one may creatively give form to things that are at hand.

Like sculptors shall they shape their own existence, and, by setting an example, they will show to those around them how one creates a life that truly is worth living.

To be sure, they may not find too many who will follow their example; yet everyone whom their experience can instruct will thus be "cured" and, through the same experience, will in turn cure others. And in this way they help reduce the ailing cells within the organism that embraces all mankind.

TRULY, THERE IS urgent need to work for the recovery of the unhealthy cells in mankind's spiritual organism; and every individual is obligated to pursue this goal as best he can.

Every human being has for aeons borne the burden of a personal guilt, a debt that waits to be redeemed; given that all things that are defective, ill, and crippled in mankind's spiritual body as a whole were caused collectively by each and everyone; namely, at the instant of that "origin," that cosmic "fall" when mankind severed the connection with its life in God.

All infinities of the material universe could be a garden of ineffable serenity and bliss—if that original separation had not taken place; and aeons need to pass before that rift can once again be healed.

But even in this present age, on our journey through those aeons, the earth could know far greater happiness than mankind realizes or is willing to believe; although, within this cosmic epoch, life on earth will never be like "heaven."

THERE IS NO NEED to search for new external forms to organize the life of states and peoples if the abundant happiness potentially existing on this earth is ever to become a living fact.

All external structures of community are merely surrogates we feel impelled to build, urged by a subconscious sense of our inner unity in mankind's spiritual body, lest we completely lose the feeling of our oneness in the Spirit's world.

The sense of unity that still reveals itself in the establishment of states, in nations, or in ethnic groups, is but the consciousness of being part of individual "limbs" belonging to the body as a whole. For those, however, who cannot yet perceive themselves as parts and centers of mankind's all-embracing spiritual body, it may initially suffice if they at least can feel connected to such "limbs," and thus not be detached completely from the unity and inner life of mankind's comprehensive organism.

Utter folly, however, and tantamount to self-defilement is all contempt and hatred among the sundry limbs comprising mankind as a whole.

It is the stench of putrefaction that issues from the hatred toward each other of any such infected limbs.

Without exception it betrays corruption and decay of the component cells.

At times it also is the pestilential odor of a sore that festers on an ailing limb and threatens to consume its very life.

"Whoever shows no honor to a stranger, or to a member of another tribe, does not deserve to call himself the son of a respected people" is a maxim of discerning Eastern wisdom which, inspired by enlightened knowledge, sought to teach its people self-respect.

You cannot feel true self-respect, however, unless you comprehend your full responsibility; but you can never know your full responsibility unless you realize that, as a part of mankind's spiritual organism, you are accountable not only to yourself, but also to that body as a whole.

By virtue of creating happiness in your own life you tangibly increase the sum of happiness experienced on this earth. And thereby you accomplish more for mankind as a whole than by attempting to establish in your outer world the most beguiling of utopian theories.

Meng-tzu said, "To do the right thing means to concentrate on things that are at hand; but everyone is looking for something far away. To act correctly means accomplishing what can be easily achieved; but all are searching for attainments that are difficult."

Perhaps you, too, are still consumed by the idea of having to accomplish something "great" and thus are searching for achievements that are very difficult. And so you follow lofty aims outside yourself, while your sublimest goal could not, indeed, be closer, because it rests within you.

GUIDE YOURSELF to knowledge, and you will be a guide for others by setting an example; not by usurping an authority that no one ever gave you.

Create the happiness you seek in your own life, and those around you shall discover theirs. You thus will best prepare the way to happiness for "all mankind."

Yet to achieve the happiness that you desire

you need to, with unflagging energy, sustain your faith in the inevitable victory of what is good; despite all the destructiveness and evil you might see around you.

Never must you lose your courage, however dark and menacing the clouds might seem that gather now and then above your head.

BEING ILL, exert your faith to make you well. And if your life can still be saved, then the physicians in whose skill you put your trust will thank you for assisting them in expediting your recovery. However, if one can no longer save your life, your faith will have provided you a source of inner energies that will enrich your spiritual organism once you have discarded the material body that has caused you pain.

If you have need of life's necessities, exert your faith to generate material help; and ceaselessly employ all means to keep your faith alive and active until assistance has arrived. At the same time, however, quietly pursue all the external ways you think most likely to provide the needed help, even without drawing on your faith.

The hidden energy of faith perhaps may merge with those external ways; however, it may just as often bring you help from a direction you did not expect.

But bear in mind that putting trust in the dynamic power of your faith must never tempt you passively to wait and merely hope; just as, in the case of illness, you must at no time shun the help that you are offered through external means.

Your faith would lose the life of its dynamic force unless you concentrated, at the same time, all of your other energies on the desired goal. And even though assistance were finally to reach you from an unsuspected source, making it appear as if your outside efforts had not been essential, you must not let this tempt you, in a future instance, to neglect employing all external means at your disposal.

You would regret it bitterly not to have made

this effort, because the energy inherent in your faith cannot become effective if you do not exert all of your other faculties as well.

Failure to engage all given energies will cause your faith to be as soft as lead. Yet actively employing—for all your confidence in faith—every ounce of strength you find within you in your daily life, and using it to help yourself, will let your faith become like tempered steel: an indestructible "Toledo," which is not shattered even on the hardest rock, and ultimately cuts apart the tangled knot that cannot be unraveled any other way.

In EVERY KIND of worry or distress you should be guided by these very rules if you would test the hidden power of your faith within your daily life.

Most people are unable effectively to use the energy of faith because on one occasion or another they had without success attempted to compel this hidden energy to serve them, while neglecting at the same time to make every effort to obtain assistance from without.

As a result, they make the opposite mistake, in that they now rely completely on external things. And so they toil and strain with little success, merely because at one time they had failed in their attempt to use the highest force potentially at their command, and therefore have no longer any confidence in faith as a creative energy.

It is but lack of insight into the inherent principles of spiritual laws that keeps most people from establishing their happiness in life securely, and on the basis of such laws.

Thus it happens that they feel excluded from ever knowing any happiness in life, and in this frame of mind all happiness indeed will shun them.

If you intend to build your happiness upon a sound foundation you must possess unshakeable and "optimistic" faith, both in your own good fortune and in your given right to happiness.

You need to recognize that by your striving after happiness in every just and proper way you only do what is your duty, and that your happiness can truly be far greater than the pleasures of the common herd.

From all things you encounter you must try to gain a particle, however small, of happiness, while seeking to interpret everything that happens to you in your favor.

From dawn to dusk you must not let the smallest matter cross your path from which you fail to strike at least a tiny spark of happiness.

All things your senses may perceive must offer you some little "tribute" toward your happiness, and you must grow so used to finding happiness wherever you may turn that it will seem quite natural if one day you experience a truly singular good fortune.

Without developing the habit of your wanting to discover happy fortune everywhere and in all kinds of ways, even in the smallest form, you are not able to create the very atmosphere you need to make your life on earth a work of lasting happiness.

You must become a magnet, as it were, that will attract good fortune both to yourself and others, if you would soon and without disappointments make yourself the author of your happiness on earth.

In other words, you must have learned already to be happy in a passive way before you actively begin to shape the kind of happiness that you desire.

Thus you will effect within yourself a state of mind and soul in which you shall intuitively comprehend the hidden spiritual laws by which all happiness is governed.

You then are certain to create your happiness in life, and will know how to keep it. At the same time, however, you thus increase the possibility that also others shall secure the greatest happiness this present life holds out to them, but which they cannot find because they do not realize that happiness is something which they must themselves create.

No MISFORTUNE in this world, in which adversity abounds, is so immense that it could hold good fortune back forever.

But with every instance of good fortune that you consciously perceive as happiness you stop another of the countless sources adding misery to life on earth. And once you have in fact created your own enduring happiness, you shall have rid the earth forever of one of the innumerable swamps of grief, which ignorance and thoughtlessness have bred throughout the ages, and which no power can lay dry except the energy of many "suns": of individuals who found their happiness within.

The more that kind of truly happy individual shall grow in strength and number, the weaker shall become the force of chaos on this planet's face, where to this day it still accounts for so much grief.

ATTEMPTING TO eliminate the world's afflictions any other way would merely be the wasted toil of Sisyphus, because all human fortune, be it happiness or misery, is but the last effect of spiritual laws. One has to recognize, however, that the hidden cosmic forces that automatically bring forth, in every realm of this material universe, what we on earth experience as "misfortune" shall never be immobilized, unless the energies that emanate from happiness become so powerful by being constantly experienced—as coils of copper wire will intensify electric current—that they can turn the energies producing negative events into the opposite direction. And now these very energies will just as automatically be forced to serve the goals of mankind in constructive ways.

NOT EVEN THE collective will of mankind as a whole is strong enough to stop and redirect all the destructive elements at work throughout the universe, and their effect would be experienced by humanity even if the possibility existed to gain control of all the forces causing grief and damage on this planet.

Still, in this present life, and on the earth he now inhabits, every individual is capable of working nearly "miracles" if by his own free will he shall make happiness his foremost goal. And as increasing numbers of human beings practice to achieve that end, more and more are bound to find their happiness and thus will serve as magnets of good fortune.

But since all life throughout creation is connected, intimately linked by mystery-enshrouded energies, the consequences of substantially increasing happiness on earth are bound to manifest themselves through the entire universe. And no imagination, however bold and vivid, could approach reality if one should seek to picture the effects that a dramatic rise of consciously experienced happiness on earth would have in even the most distant reaches of creation.

CONCLUSION

THE FEW IN EVERY generation who knew about and lived according to the laws described in the foregoing pages had been prevented long enough from speaking of their knowledge to anyone except their tried and tested pupils. In the course of thousands of years they found abundant opportunity to trace the workings of these laws through all their final consequences, and to witness their effectiveness both on themselves and in the lives of others.

This is guidance you may safely trust. And if you wish to find out more about its source and nature, my *Book on the Living God* *, *The Book on Life Beyond* *, *The Book on Man*, as

* Available in English, see Appendix.

well as *The Book on the Royal Art* and *The Book of Dialogues*, will offer you the needed background in detail.

I here conclude this *Book on Happiness* with the sincere hope that it will help you find the way by which you shall yourself become the author of your happiness on earth.

Much more, indeed, could still be said about the countless forms of happiness you can experience in this life, and you will not, I trust, assume that there is any kind of happiness I might have overlooked, because it is not mentioned in this book.

If you can read the way one ought to read you will find guidance that applies to every kind of happiness you may encounter in this life.

My purpose here was only to present, in the briefest manner possible, the essential laws you need to bear in mind, in that they underlie all forms of happiness on earth without exception. I merely chose a few examples that lent themselves especially well to demonstrating what these present expositions on human happiness would have you understand. It was my goal to be as clear as possible, and thus I was not able to avoid all repetitions.

The task I set myself, however, was to use the fewest pages, and still discuss all topics I considered to have value for your better understanding of the subject.

I WOULD NOT have you read my books like novels, which are laid aside the moment one has reached the final page, and which are then perhaps not opened in this life again.

I know of many to whom my books already have become reliable companions in their lives, and so I hope that many more shall make them such in future.

But while each book I wrote is meant to serve its reader as a constant guide, I nonetheless especially would hope the present *Book on Happiness* might never leave the reader's side. For if in other books I deal with matters that frequently transcend concerns of daily life, I here have stated much, I think, for which each day may bring occasion to look into the book again in order to acquaint oneself completely with its contents.

This certainly will not be to your disadvantage; indeed, it well might gradually transform you, despite the many problems you must face in outer life, into a solid optimist; even though today you still may think that pessimism is the only true philosophy.

You must not be misled, however, by those who would convince you, by example of their own "experience," that happiness will simply shun the lives of certain individuals, despite their constant efforts to attain it.

People whose experience inspires that belief should rather ask themselves how they had, by their own mistakes, prevented happiness from entering their lives.

Perhaps they ought to question whether their

excessive busyness was not in fact the cause why happiness has fled them.

To be sure, all happiness on earth must be created. But quietly creating inner joy is very different from the anxiety and constant worry of one who fears there might be something he has overlooked, and thereby loses the most precious gift: that calm serenity within the soul which is the very key to any form of happiness on earth.

SECURE WITHIN yourself a cheerful certainty, convinced that happiness is yours by right, and let no setback ever drive you from the stronghold of your firmly anchored faith.

Rest assured, there are at all times energies at work that offer you their help the moment you are truly willing to create the happiness you seek, instead of only longing for it, full of hopes and wishes.

Calmly go the way on which you have been placed on earth, and always guard your inner peace, no matter how the "blows of fate" might thunder all around you.

If one can tear you from the stronghold of your inner peace, you will most certainly be lost. Know , however, that the forces that produce ill fortune in this life can never really defeat you so long as you, with steadfast, quiet trust, put all your faith in your good fortune, and in the inner powers that support you with their help.

With patience and some practice you will no doubt be able to create the happiness that you desire, even though today you still might be besieged by many things that make you feel unhappy.

Distrust the fables other "doctrines" might be telling you about the dearth of happiness supposedly encumbering this planet.

Trust, instead your own good right—indeed, your moral duty—to experience lasting happiness; and strive, with firm resolve and confident serenity, truly to create it in your life: so that you, too, may one day find yourself among this planet's *happy* guests.

REMINDER

"Yet here I must point out again that if one would derive the fullest benefit from studying the books I wrote to show the way into the Spirit, one has to read them in the original; even if this should require learning German.

"Translations can at best provide assistance in helping readers gradually perceive, even through the spirit of a different language, what I convey with the resources of my mother tongue."

From "Answers to Everyone" (1933), *Gleanings.* Bern: Kobersche Verlagsbuchhandlung, 1990.

ALSO AVAILABLE FROM
THE KOBER PRESS:

Bô Yin Râ
The Book on the Living God

Contents: Word of Guidance. "The Tabernacle of God is with Men." The "Mahatmas" of Theosophy. Meta-Physical Experiences. The Inner Journey. The En-Sof. On Seeking God. On Leading an Active Life. On "Holy Men" and "Sinners." The Hidden Side of Nature. The Secret Temple. Karma. War and Peace. The Unity Among Religions. The Will to Find Eternal Light. Mankind's Higher Faculties of Knowing. On Death. On the Spirit's Radiant Substance. The Path Toward Perfection. On Everlasting Life. The Spirit's Light Dwells in the East. Faith, Talismans, and Images of God. The Inner Force in Words. A Call from Himavat. Giving Thanks. Epilogue.

The Kober Press, 1991. 333 pages, paperback. ISBN 0-915034-03-4.

In this central work of *The Enclosed Garden*—Bô Yin Râ's thirty-two-volume cycle on questions of religion, ethics, and philosophy seen from a spiritual perspective—the author clarifies a number of perplexing concepts that still are subject to much speculation.

By drawing clear distinctions between the real substance of those concepts and their fictional accretions, the author furnishes the needed touchstone that will let the reader disentangle truth from fiction in questions of religious faith. And this alone can prove a liberating inspiration for those who would explore objective knowledge.

Bô Yin Râ
The Book on Life Beyond

Contents: Introduction. The Art of Dying. The Temple of Eternity and the World of Spirit. The Only Absolute Reality. What Should One Do?

The Kober Press, 1978. 115 pages, paperback. ISBN 0-915034-02-6.

In this objective presentation of human life as it will be experienced after death—without the benefits and disadvantages of a material body—the author shows that mortal life, from the perspective of eternity, appears as but a brief, yet very consequential, interruption of a state of being which in fact is timeless. In particular, the author explains why "incarnation" can normally occur no more than once—excepting suicide, death in infancy, and pathological compulsion toward material life—and why this life on earth has such far-reaching consequences for the human being's spiritual condition in the life to come.

A sobering note for readers fascinated by "occult" phenomena will be the author's explanation that the few authentic cases of such contact, far from revealing anything spiritual, are purely physical, involving nature's hidden side, and that all probing in this realm is harmful for the physical and psychological well-being of the individual.

The Book on Life Beyond is meant to serve its readers as a "guidebook" that describes realities they may expect to find in life beyond, and also will instruct them how this present life can best prepare them to approach the life to come with peace of mind and inner joy.

Bô Yin Râ
The Wisdom of St. John

Contents: Introduction. The Master's Image. The Luminary's Mortal Life. The Aftermath. The Missive. The Authentic Doctrine. The Paraclete. Conclusion.

The Kober Press, 1975. 92 Pages, clothbound. ISBN 0-915034-01-8.

First published in 1924, long before the last recurrent spate of interest in the historical life and teachings of Jesus of Nazareth, this work restores the actual events surrounding his existence, death, and doctrine as witnessed by his own contemporaries.

Separating truth from fiction, while giving a profounder meaning to some ancient myths, the book reveals a more majestic, but at the same time more convincing image of the Son of Man than has been fashioned by belief and dogma.

The author stresses that the key to understanding the real substance of the gospel message lies in knowing what Jesus meant when speaking of his "Father"—whom tradition would mistakenly confuse with "God"—or of his "brothers," of the "Son of Man," the "prince of this world," or of the "Comforter."

The spiritual perspective of the author shows this text to be unique among the gospel records as it alone contains authentic fragments of instruction written by the Master for his pupils to remind them of his words.

Bô Yin Râ
About My Books; Concerning My Name; and Other Texts

Contents: Foreword. About My Books. Concerning My Name. In My Own Behalf. Important Difference. Résumé. Comments on the Cycle *The Enclosed Garden* and the Related Works. The Works of Bô Yin Râ. Brief Biography of Bô Yin Râ. Frontispiece: photographic portrait of the author.

The Kober Press, 1977. 67 pages, paperback. ISBN 0-915034-00-X

As its contents indicate, this collection of short articles, excerpts, and quotations is intended as a general introduction to the works and background of the writer, painter, and interpreter of inner life who signed his works as "Bô Yin Râ," a proper name, expressing in phonetic symbols what he experienced as his spiritual identity.

The selection gathered in this little volume will let the readers gain a clear conception of the substance, purpose, and perspective of the author's expositions. It thus provides them with an overview on a substantial body of work that is only now being made available in English. In addition, the present pages offer practical criteria to discern the spiritual credentials and authority of anyone who speaks or writes on final things.

THE
KOBER
PRESS